ODUU LAKKOOFSOTOOTAA

THE NUMBER STORY

SMALL BOOK ONE

ENGLISH - OROMO

Numbers Teach Children
Their Number Names

written and illustrated by

MISS ANNA

Early Reader Edition of *The Number Story 1*
Bronze Medal Winner, 2016 Wishing Shelf Book Award

Library of Congress Control Number: 2018902040

Names: Miss Anna, author.
Title: Number story : numbers teach children their number names / Miss Anna.
Description: Portland, OR: Lumpy Publishing, 2018.
Identifiers: ISBN 978-1-945977-68-8 | LCCN 2018902040
Summary: The pictures and rhymes present stories which introduce numbers 0-10.
Subjects: LCSH Numeration—English--Oromo--Pictorial works--Juvenile literature. | BISAC JUVENILE NONFICTION /
Languages: English--Oromo
Classification: LCC QA141.3 .M57 2018 | DDC 513—dc23

Publisher: Lumpy Publishing
Website: www.missannabooks.com
Email: missanna@missannabooks.com

Paperback: ISBN 978-1-945977-68-8
Printed in the U.S.A.   1 3 5 7 9 10 8 6 4 2

Maqaa lakkoofsotaa
baruu feetaa?

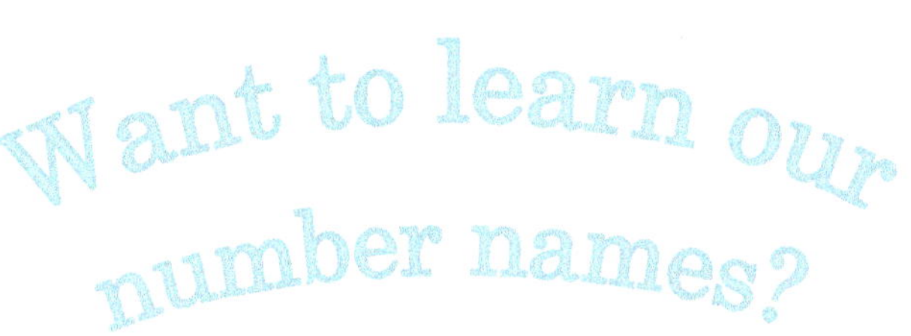

It is very easy and a lot of fun!

Baay'ee salphaa fi kan
nama booharsuu dha!

Say-along our little jingle

Nu wajjiin weeddisi!

starting from Number One!

Lakkoofsa tokkoffaa irraa haa eegallu!

1
ONE looks like my one finger.
TOKKO
Quba koo fakkaata.

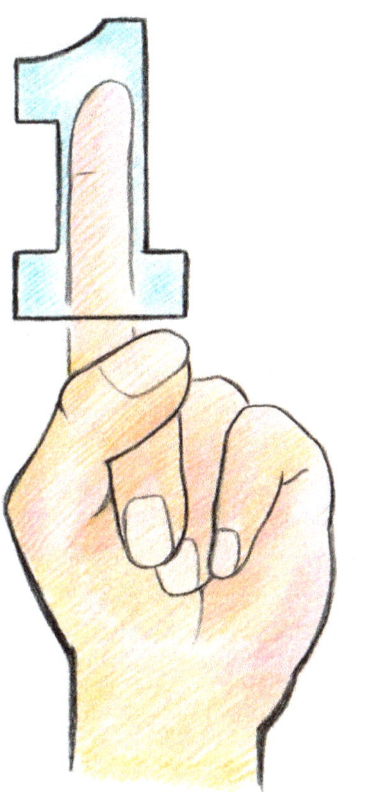

ONE!

TOKKO!

2
TWO trails a tail.
LAMA
Eegee qaba.

A TAIL! EEGEE!

3

THREE   has bumps.

SADI

Quutaa qaba.

BUMPY! QUUTAA LAALI!

4

FOUR carries a sail.

AFUR

Darbata qaba.

A SAIL!
DARBATA DOONII!

5

FIVE   is a racing track.

SHAN

Karaa dorgommii
konkolaataa ti.

VROOM
CHUU!

6

SIX   curves like a snail.

JAHA

Akka Qocaa ofirra deebi'a.

A SNAIL!   QOCAA!

7

OUCH!

A!

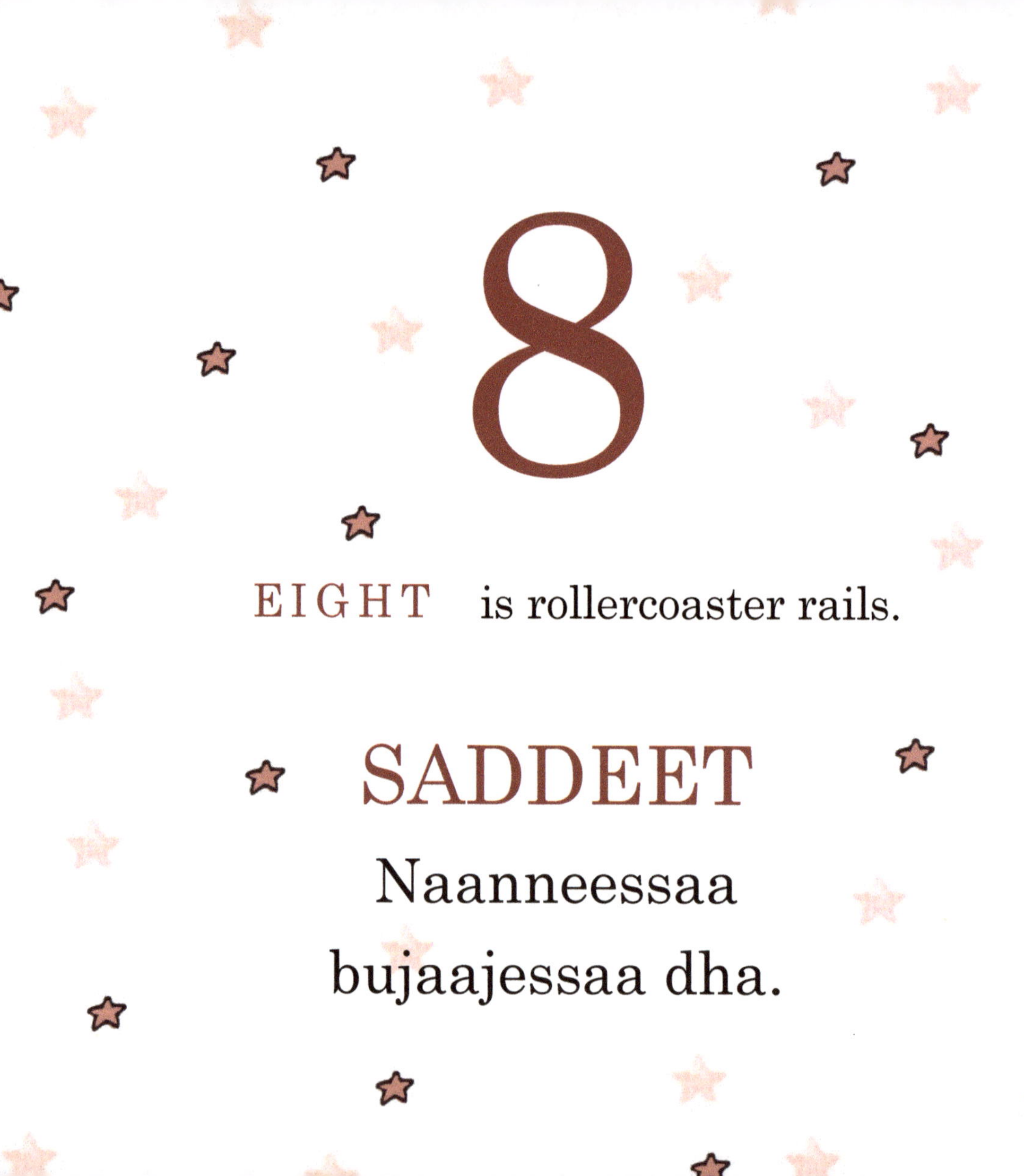

8

EIGHT   is rollercoaster rails.

SADDEET
Naanneessaa
bujaajessaa dha.

OYYAA!
YIPPEE!

9

NINE   is a bubble on a stick.

SAGAL

Hoomacha mukarraa ti.

A BUBBLE! AFUUFFAA!

10

TEN   is an eye of a whale.

KUDHAN

Ija tokkicha qurxummii.

HELLO!
AS LAAL!

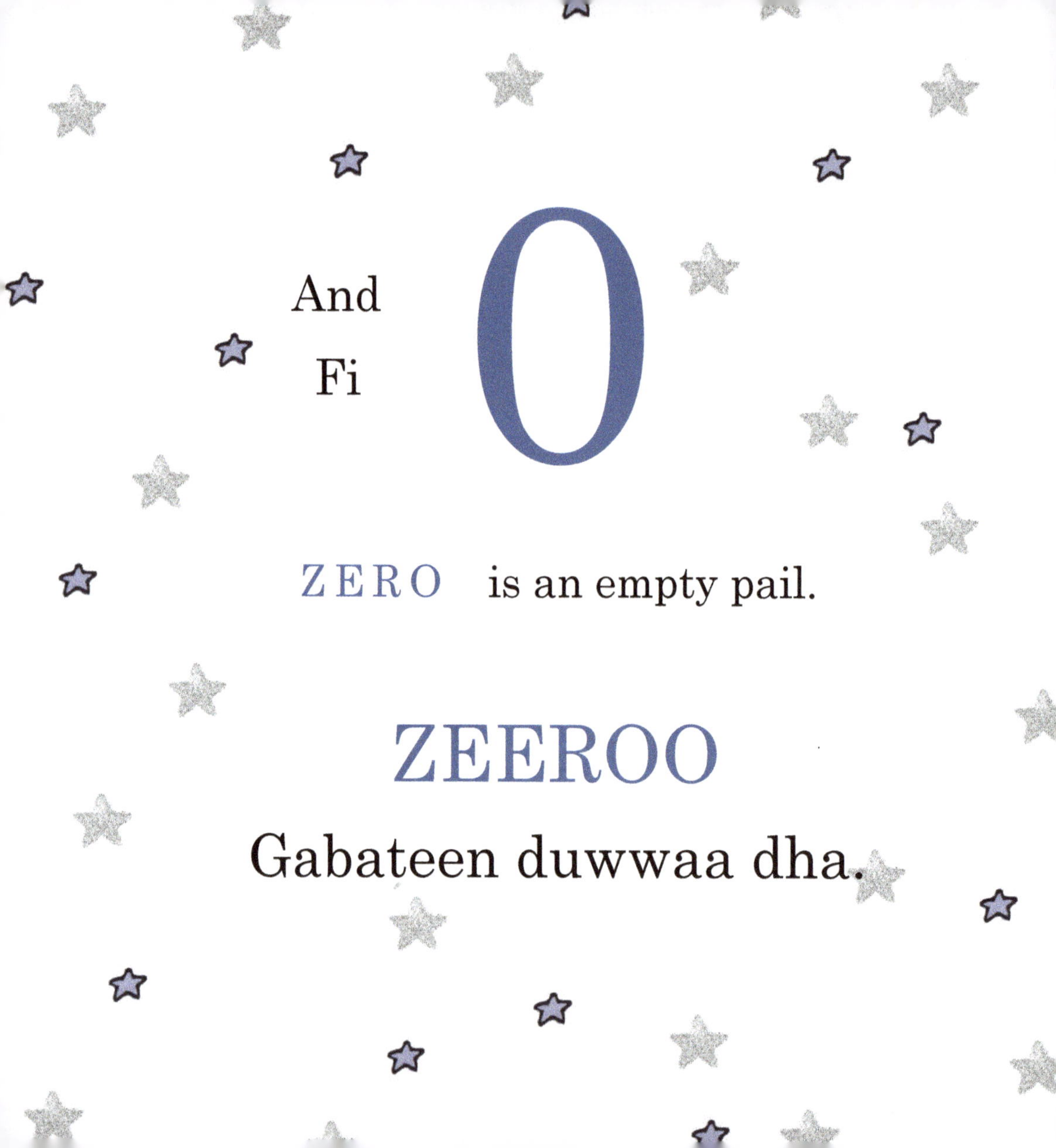
And
Fi

0

ZERO is an empty pail.

ZEEROO

Gabateen duwwaa dha.

IT'S EMPTY!
DUWWAA DHA!

Thank you for playing with us today.

We had a lot of fun too!

Harra nu wajjiin taphachuu
keetiif galatoomi.
Nu'is baay'ee gammanne!

We are your Number friends,
Zero to Ten,
Who will be here for you~
Nu'i hiriyyoota kee Lakkoofsota
Zeeroo irraa hanga kudhanii.
Asuma sumaan wajjiin jirra~

Bye-bye now!
See you again soon!
Ammaaf nagaatti!
Wal garra!

The Numbers are *SINGING* too!

To sing-a-long, look for Miss Anna Number Story
at your favorite music store like iTUNES.

MP3

Numbers 0-10
IDENTIFYING & COUNTING

Numbers 11-20
& Ordinals
first, second, third...

Numbers 0-100
& Place Values
ones, tens, hundreds...

About Clocks
& Telling Time
hours, minutes, seconds

Number Story 1 & 2
isbn: 978-0-996216-48-7

Number Story 3 & 4
isbn: 978-1-945977-01-5

Number Story 5 & 6
isbn: 978-1-945977-06-0

Number Story 7 & 8
isbn: 978-1-949320-40-4

For more Miss Anna books to love,
visit us at

www.missannabooks.com

Numbers are working hard all over the world!
Come Travel the World with Us!